Book 3

A Logical Approach to Spelling

Highly structured curriculum based on the sounds in words and the application of spelling rules.

Jurina Dean

Thank you

The journey continues...

I want to extend a big thank you to my three older children for engaging with my books, even though you've already passed this spelling stage. Lamonie thank you for drawing on demand! You are a star. Jemimah, your excitement and love for your Mamma's books mean the world to me. And to my husband, thank you for your unwavering support throughout this journey. Love you all dearly!

Index

Preface

Welcome to the journey of helping your child learn to read and write in English! I invite you to pause and take a moment to explore this preface, as it sets the stage for the incredible impact this book can have on your child's learning experience.

As a mother of four living in Geneva, Switzerland, I understand the unique challenges and opportunities that come with raising children in a multi language environment. My eldest daughter breezed through her weekly spelling lists, effortlessly mastering each word. However, my second daughter faced a different path. The frustration she experienced with her spelling lists was palpable. While she could learn words, recalling them a week later felt like an insurmountable task.

After discovering that she had dyslexia and short-term verbal memory challenges, I embarked on a five-year journey of learning and discovering how to work through the curriculum using an alternative method.

I was advised to focus on the 300 most frequently used words in English. We dedicated a year to mastering these words, achieving a 50% success rate. While this was a start, I knew there had to be a better way. My daughter excelled in math, successfully following logical steps to solve problems. This inspired me to research a logical approach to spelling.

In my quest to find effective resources, I explored many different books and countless online materials. I realised that a vast amount of these resources lacked the structure and repetition necessary for lasting retention.

While I couldn't find a single definitive resource, I began piecing together a beautiful method for learning to spell in English—one that emphasises a logical structure, much like maths. This book aims to provide that framework.

In English spelling, we often encounter exceptions to the rule, but we'll tackle these later in our journey. Initially, we focus on what makes sense phonetically and explore homophones as a key theme throughout this book. Together, we'll play detective, investigating the fascinating world of different spellings. As a child's brain develops, they will naturally anchor these "exception to the rule" words.

Our curriculum provides a strong foundation and support for visual memory and logical thinking. We cover all spelling elements of national curriculums, but with a difference — we emphasise the sounds in words and foster confidence in blending simple words for future success.

We'll explore "borrowed" words from other languages, highlighting the similarities that can serve as helpful anchors. Towards the end of the series, we'll address words that often cause confusion early on for children who find spelling challenging. These words will align correctly in your child's mind as they mature, so we won't focus on teaching them prematurely. Instead, we'll nurture their spelling confidence in stages of mind-readiness.

At the end of each section, you'll find a word bank. Use this to create spelling tests until your child masters each word, revisiting it throughout the series. Be mindful of your child's attention span, and keep lessons between 10 to 30 minutes a day. Consistent, short repetitions are key! Help them understand why words are spelled a certain way, and revisit the word bank after a month, and again after three months.

You are making a wonderful difference to your child's learning journey! Enjoy every moment of this experience—it truly passes quickly. Happy learning together!

Reading and Spelling - Book Three

Let us start our exciting journey in Book 3! We've explored all the sounds of vowels and consonants, blending them together, and discovering the various vowel combinations and names. We've also learned about "illegal" letters at the end of words and had a look at syllables in Book 2. We've touched on the basics of the floss rule and when to use c, k, and ck. Now, we're ready to dive into some more challenging and rewarding concepts. In Book 3, we will explore c & g in depth, focusing on their loud and soft sounds. We'll also cover plural and past tense words, comparative and superlative forms, contractions, and even some silent letters that we write but don't hear.

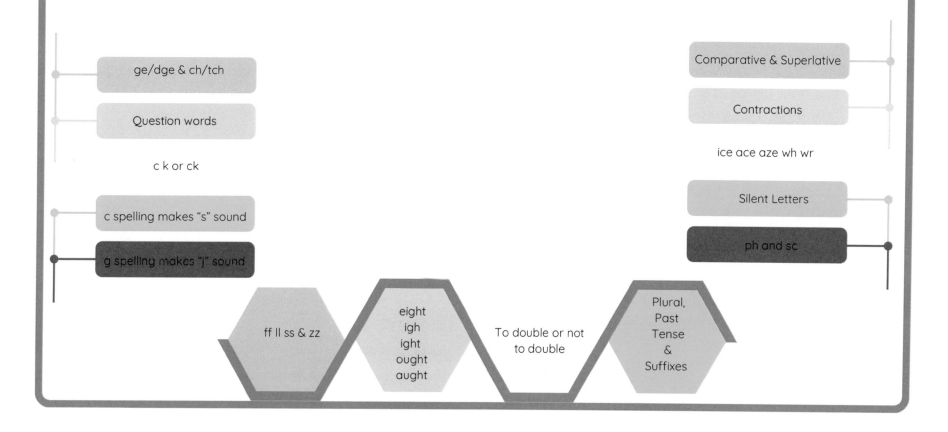

ge/dge & ch/tch

Question words

c k or ck

c spelling makes "s" sound

g spelling makes "j" sound

ff ll ss & zz

eight
igh
ight
ought
aught

To double or not to double

Plural, Past Tense & Suffixes

Comparative & Superlative

Contractions

ice ace aze wh wr

Silent Letters

ph and sc

Tips

You may be picking up this book as the first one in the series. Often when children find this level challenging, it is because too much confusion crept in at the earlier stages of learning to spell. I encourage you to review book one and two with them. This will eradicate some of the frustrations that have built up because too much was introduced too soon for them.

It's important to take things step by step! First, let's focus on mastering the sounds of the alphabet before introducing their names. This will help build a strong foundation for blending sounds as we read and write. Once your child is confident with the sounds, we can gently introduce the five vowel names (like a for acorn). Remember, knowing the ABC song isn't necessary for learning to read or write; understanding the sounds each letter makes is key.

As we progress, let's ensure your child is comfortable with small letters before moving on to capital letters. Capital letters are special and are mainly used for names and at the beginning of sentences.

When it comes to print and cursive letters, let's take our time! Mastering print letters first will help avoid confusion, especially with letters like b and d.

Happy Spelling!
Jurina Dean

What a typical week with this book looks like

Daily practice in reading, writing, and spelling is essential, and it should be fun! Pay attention to your child's span and adjust as needed. Think of their attention span as a muscle that we're gradually strengthening. We can create a consistent structure for lessons or mix things up based on your child's energy and mood. On some days, starting with a spelling test followed by new activities can work well. Reading should ideally be a separate session, especially if it's longer than ten minutes. Let's keep lessons short—no more than 30 minutes without reading.

Make sure to celebrate each achievement, no matter how small! Remember, the key is to review concepts regularly and keep the learning experience joyful.

To summarise

- Learning a concept once a week, reviewing it daily
- Spelling test 20-30 words (To succeed, you have to write short spelling tests at least twice a week.)
- Exercises
- Reading 10-30 mins a day

a apple

f fan

jam j

nose

rabbit

van

b boot

g goat

whale

c cat

k kick

orange

snake

w

d doorknob and the door

horse

l leaf

pen

tail

x-ray

eggs

igloo

m mum

quick

yo-yo

zoo

It is important not to say the name of the letter, but the sound it makes! Not "A" for acorn but "a" for apple.

umbrella

a b c d e f g h i j k l m n o p q r s t u v w x y z

The "a" for apple -   says its name "A"   acorn

The "u" for umbrella - says its name "U"   uniform

The "i" for igloo - says its name "I"   item

The "e" for egg - says its name "E"   email

The "o" for orange - says its name "O"   oh!

Practice this!!!
Refer to the ABC
song here...

The "y" is our cameleon. It changes colour.
Sometimes it is a vowel like the a u i e o and
other times it prefers to be a consonant.

Often the "y" helps out the "i".

Our other good helper is the "e"
"e" comes to the rescue, when we are in a
sticky situation.

"illegal" letters at the end of a word

illegal letters

5 letters that are not permitted to be at the end of a word in English......

i   j   q   p   u   v

➡️

"e" & **"y"**
to come to the **rescue**!

➡️

- i (pi   pi**e**)
- j (oranj   oran**ge**)
- q (plaq   plaqu**e**)
- u (tru   tru**e**)
- v (giv   giv**e** lov   lov**e**)
- tri   tr**y**
- plai   pla**y**

We have covered this in the previous book. This "rule" help to explain why we spell certain words a certain way. We will refer back to these "illegal" letters often.

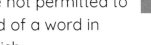

The "y" is our cameleon. It changes colour. Sometimes it is a vowel like the a u i e o and other times it prefers to be a consonant.

Often the "y" helps out the "i".

Our other good helper is the "e"
"e" comes to the rescue, when we are in a sticky situation.

Illegal letters

5 letters that are not permitted to be at the end of a word in English......

i j q p u v

We rely on the letter "**e**" & "**y**" to come to the **rescue**!

- i (pi   pi**e**)
- j (oranj   orang**e**)
- q (plaq   plaqu**e**)
- u (tru   tru**e**)
- v (giv   giv**e** lov   lov**e**)

illegal letters
...that is why....

tri	try	hav	have
fri	fry	abov	above
unti	untie	weav	weave
		lov	love
tru	true		
glu	glue	uniq	unique
		arrang	arrange

soft "g" = j

Oooooopppppssss!

There will always be exceptions ....but we are learning the general pattern first

Exceptions: menu flu fungi ski hi ... a lot of these are what we like to call "borrowed" words from other languages, cultures, fashions, science, abbreviations or even slang (informal speech).

Vowels

Every word must have a vowel
&
Every syllable must have a vowel

a   e   i   o   u

& "chameleon" y

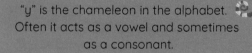

"y" is the chameleon in the alphabet. Often it acts as a vowel and sometimes as a consonant.

- Letter **sounds** are different from letter **names**
- Every vowel letter can be associated with at least 2 sounds!
- SHORT SOUND   **SOUND**
  a e o u i
- LONG SOUND   **NAME**
  (says its name A E O U I)
  We refer to the name of the letter by putting it in brackets
  {A} {E} {O} {U} {I}

Long vowel sounds - Diphthongs - Revision

When two vowels go walking, the first one does the
talking   ...it says its name

a + i   ai {A}
a + y   ay {A}

- train
- brain
- pay
- clay

When two vowels go walking, the first one does the
talking   ...it says its name

o + e   oe {O}
o + a   oa {O}

- toe
- foe
- goat
- float

foe or friend

For a short vowel sound to say its name, you can add an "e" on the end of a word

a _ e   {A}   • brak   • brake
e _ e   {E}   • delet   • delete
o _ e   {O}   • brok   • broke
i _ e   {I}   • strik   • strike
u _ e   {U}   • flut   • flute

When two vowels go walking, the first one does the
talking   ...it says its name

e + a   ea {E}
e + e   ee {E}
e + y   ey {E}
e + i   ei {E}

- team
- green
- honey
- sheik

When two vowels go walking, the first one does the
talking   ...it says its name

i + e   ie {I}

- tie
- pie
- die

When two vowels go walking, the first one does the
talking   ...says its name

u + e   ue {U}
u + i   ui {U}

- glue
- true
- fruit

...ge or...dge???   ...ch or ...tch???

  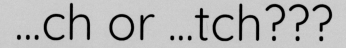 

huge   **lodge**   **punch**   **match**

- a <u>SHORT</u> vowel sound with the [dge/tch] sound at the end, **we write <u>ALL</u> the letters dge/tch**
- a <u>LONG</u> vowel sound with the [dge/tch] sound at the end, **we write <u>ONLY</u> the letters ge/ch**

short
a e o i u
sound

⬇

**-dge
-tch**

long
{A} {E} {O} {I} {U}
sound

⬇

**-ge
-ch**

 *think about it like this*

There is a long sound, let us add only a couple of letters OR that is a super short sound, let us add a lot of letters!

short sound + -dge -tch

hatch	witch*	blotchy
match	switch	scratchy
snatch	sketch	
scratch	clutch	• blotchy....at end the of word we hear an [E] sound, so we add a "y" for it.
patch	crutch	
stitch	twitch	
hitch		

edge	nudge	merge
hedge	smudge	verge
ledge	grudge	forge
wedge	judge	gorge
pledge	fridge	stage
sledge	bridge	barge
dodge	ridge	large
lodge		charge
stodge		urge
budge		purge
fudge		surge

belch	bunch
bench	lunch
clench	munch
drench	punch
inch	stench
flinch	pinches
pinch	rich

binge	
cringe	
plunge	
lounge	
twinge	
strange	
range	
change	
orange	

long sound + -ge -ch

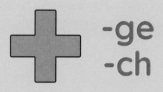

rich

- Sometimes there are a **cheeky "n", "r" or "l"** in the word. Be careful...there is now "enough" letters, so we just add "ch" or "ge"!
- As you progress, add -es -ed -ing etc. to words.
- EXCEPTION to learn: **much** and **such**

- Ask ridge/rich and witch/which together and talk about the meaning of these words. If you know another language, ie french...the word in french for rich is "riche"....so with no "d" sound. So we do something similar in English. Anchors ⚓ are so important to remind us how to spell words.

Homophones

ridge
rich
witch
which?

witch

ridge

Exceptions to Learn
much
such

Which witch wished she had a big nose?

dge ge tch ch

Connect the right word with the photo

much such ← Exceptions!!

hedge
ledge
wedge
pledge
sledge
dodge
lodge

fudge
nudge
judge
fridge
bridge
barge
orange

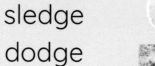
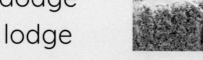
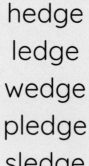

surge
cringe
plunge
lounge
merge
gorge
edge

snatch
stitch
crutch
bench
pinch
drench
stench

dge ge tch ch

Circle the letters that determines whether we add dge or ge & tch or ch.
Then connect it to the most suitable reason.

hedge

surge

lounge

ledge

wedge

merge

orange

sledge

huge

lodge

barge

refuge

fudge

LONG
VOWEL

MANY
LETTERS

SHORT
VOWEL

snatch

drench

pinch

stitch

stench

crutch

bench

pinch

Add dge ge tch or ch

sur	bin	ur
loun	ran	ca
nu	twi	sta
oran	whi	fri
sle	wi	bri
cru	crin	e
gru	twin	pun
ju	we	pin
ben	lun	do
la	ri	sna
sti	ri	fu
dren	lar	sle
plun	su	mu

Circle the correct spelling

The witch/which with her hudge/huge crooked nose/knows was sitting in her loundge/lounge. The only way to escape was over a brige/bridge and over the hege/hedge.

Not far from there lived a nigt/knight who could fight/fite in the nite/night with all his mite/might. Even in the brite/bright lite/light he could puntch/punch and scrach/scratch. The witch/wich was no mach/match for him.

I think it was her hight/height and her wait/weight that was the biggest problem. The nite/knight was only ate/eigt/eight years old. He was mutch/much younger than the strandge/strange old lady.

Answers in the back of the book.

Rewrite these sentences with the correct spelling.

Homophones 🔊👂

Learn these 4 words together. (Write "peas" 3 different ways, and tell me which one is which. Then write please.)

  Can I have a piece of cake? The strawberry is the "i" on the cake.

piece

peas

One "e" should always make peace with another "a".

peace

please

Homophones

Write these words again without looking at the previous page.

A slice of cake is called a ?

‐ ‐ ‐ ‐ ‐ ‐ ‐ ‐ ‐ ‐ ‐

Vegetables are good for you.

‐ ‐ ‐ ‐ ‐ ‐ ‐ ‐ ‐ ‐ ‐

Not war but?

‐ ‐ ‐ ‐ ‐ ‐ ‐ ‐ ‐ ‐ ‐

Remember your manners....say ?
.... and thank you.

‐ ‐ ‐ ‐ ‐ ‐ ‐ ‐ ‐ ‐ ‐

Question words
Check out the hhhhhhhhhhhh....

why? what? when? where? which?

These words we call "question words". All the question words have a "h" when we write them.
Rewrite them below on the dotted line.

t**h**ere, t**h**ey, t**h**em

w**h**ere? t**h**ere

t**h**is

w**h**at? t**h**at

t**h**ese and t**h**ose

there their they`re

They are (They're) going to their house over there, not here.

Circle the correct spelling of the word

Where/Wear are you going on holiday?

Wi/Why would you not take your teddy with you?

Wen/When will you be back?

Their/They`re/There coming with us to the beach.

Will you be going to their/there/they`re party?

Their/They`re/There are so many sports we can play on the beach.

Which/Witch/Wich of those two friends do you play ball with?

The which/wich/witch is eating her sandwitch/sandwich/sandwhich.

Tat/That is an interesting question to ask.

Their/There/They`re school is near the city.

Their/There/They`re is a big house near the school.

Rewrite these sentences with the correct spelling.

Let`s look at these words

Rewrite them on the dotted line.

could   oh (o) you (u) lucky (l) duck (d) ould

- - - - - - - - - - - - - - - - - -

would   oh (o) you (u) lucky (l) duck (d) ould

- - - - - - - - - - - - - - - - - -

should   oh (o) you (u) lucky (l) duck (d) ould

- - - - - - - - - - - - - - - - - -

tough   oh (o) you (u) grumpy (g) hamster (h)

- - - - - - - - - - - - - - - - - -

c   k   or   ck   (Revision)

BEGINNING OF A WORD

At the **BEGIN**ning of a word the "c" is a loud "k" sound if followed by....

The cat is in the cot with a cut.

a   o   u

cat   cot   cut

If we want the **BEGIN**ning of the word to be a loud "k" sound but "e" or "i" is the next letter....then the "real" "k" (also called the kicking k) comes to the rescue!

kid   kelp
kiss   Ken
kick   kennel
               Kevin

_ at   _ id

_ ot   _ en

_ ut   _ iss

_ ash   _ ennel

_ar   _elp

To make the
loud sound "k"

c + a   k + e

c + o   k + i

c + u

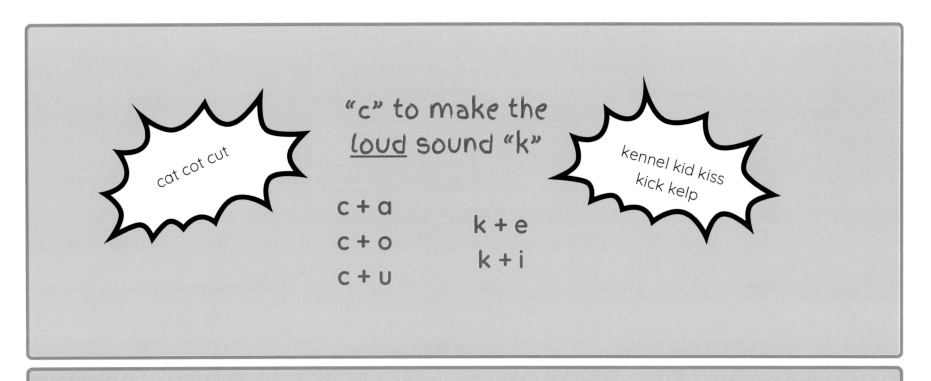

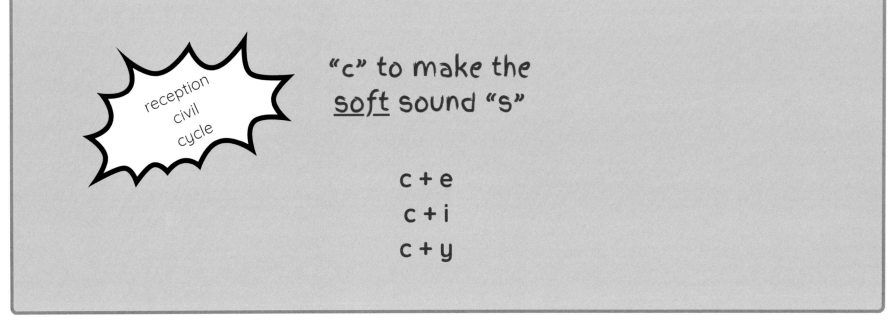

c   k   or   ck

The word is so short, let's use both the c and k!

At the **END** of a single <u>SHORT VOWEL SOUND</u> word (and mimics of it) we add CK for the loud "k" sound

p**a**ck
socks
lock
sack
backpack
rack
lack

- "a" is a short vowel sound in p**a**ck...so we add "c" & "k" = "ck"

stock
rock
suck
luck
*lucky
clock
truck
**wreck
click

- * In the word "lucky" you can hear {E} sound at the end of the word. We most often just write "y" for this sound at the end of a word

- ** w+r is a challenging sound...we will approach it later.

<u>If the vowel says it's name</u>
{A} {E} {O} {I} { U}
in the word, use the kicking "k" ONLY to say the loud "k" sound.

- The "e" letter at the end of the word, makes the vowel say its name.

fake bake brake cake
broke stroke

<u>Use ONLY "k" **AFTER** a consonant at the end of a word!</u>
pi**n**k dri**n**k bli**n**k si**n**k sha**r**k pa**r**k
da**r**k tru**n**k bla**n**k pra**n**k sa**n**k

Already enough letters.... so no need for c and k

Are these exceptions? Not really. After a consonant we use "k" for the loud sound "c".

eg. **s**kull
skunk

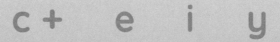

c + e i y

When "c" is written with "e" "i" or "y",
it makes a soft sound "s".

c + e   **reception**
c + i   **civil**
c + y   **cycle**

---

bicycle
recycle
cyclone
civil
cell
reception
received
princess
cell
cellphone

circus
cellar 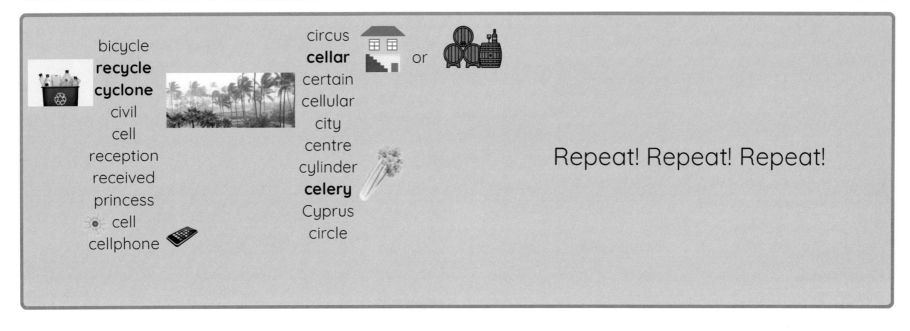 or
certain
cellular
city
centre
cylinder
celery
Cyprus
circle

Repeat! Repeat! Repeat!

Draw a line from the picture to the correct "k" sound

ck   c   k

ketchup socks cash cup car kennel sick cot kettle sack kiss lick candy kittens

"c" and "g" - loud and soft sound

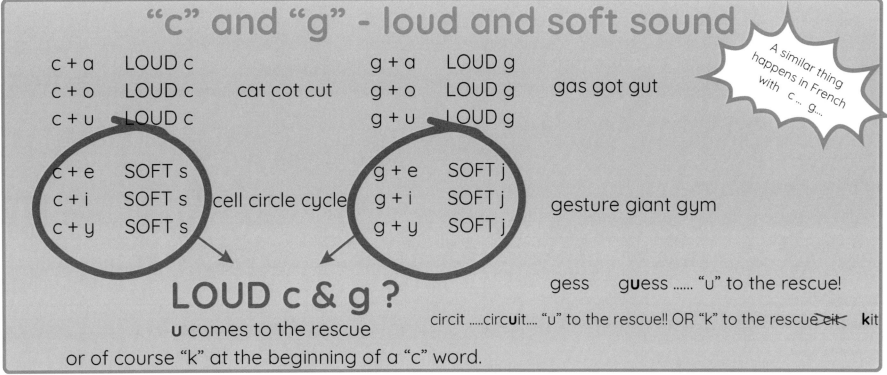

A similar thing happens in French with c ... g....

c + a   LOUD c
c + o   LOUD c   cat cot cut
c + u   LOUD c

g + a   LOUD g
g + o   LOUD g   gas got gut
g + u   LOUD g

c + e   SOFT s
c + i   SOFT s   cell circle cycle
c + y   SOFT s

g + e   SOFT j
g + i   SOFT j   gesture giant gym
g + y   SOFT j

LOUD c & g ?

u comes to the rescue

or of course "k" at the beginning of a "c" word.

gess   gu**e**ss ...... "u" to the rescue!

circit .....circ**u**it.... "u" to the rescue!! OR "k" to the rescue c̶i̶t̶ **k**it

---

c and g loud   + a o u

c and g soft   + e i y

c (loud) + e /i/y   kicking "k" to the
                rescue
                eg **k**it

c&g(loud) + e/i/y   "u" to the rescue
        eg gu**e**ss circ**u**it

SOFT sound (followed by e i y)

g**y**m
g**i**ant
g**e**sture
g**e**l
larg**e**
orang**e**

rec**e**ive
c**y**cle
fenc**e**

With the help of "**u**", "c" & "g"
becomes a **LOUD** "k" & "g"
sound

gu**e**ss
gu**e**rilla
bag**u**ette
g**u**ard
dialog**u**e
circ**u**it

Exceptions ....
get girl

Study these words and see why they are written this way.

giraffe
lar**ge**
dialo**gue**
guerilla
ba**gu**ette
cir**c**uit
circle
bis**cui**t

Put the words in the right column

- gel
- giant
- cycle
- goat
- guess
- gym
- fence
- cat
- cot
- game
- large
- rescue

loud g or c	soft g (j) or c ("s")

Word bank

rack
back
sack
backpack
lack
lick
flick
click
slick
trick
neck
suck
tuck
luck
sock
mock

can
cost
candy
cutter
canteen

vs

leek
creek
soak
bake
rake
make

kill
skill
kiss

*kit (*accent on the "t" and "d" to distinguish)
*kid
kennel

kit

kid

EXCEPTIONS

**Exceptions
to learn
here:**

skeleton
sky
ski
skunk
skull

get
gecko

giant
gel
gesture
genome
genetic
generic
gem
gender
genius
giraffe

acid
cent
cell
center
pencil
city
cycle
central
celebrate
citrus
civil

Look at the difference between
i**c**icle and pop**s**icle

C

S

bicycle

prince
prince**ss***

cyber
cymbals

prince and princess are
more challenging to write

In the words gym and bicycle you can hear the "y" is
pronounced with an "i" sound. We will look at these later.

Spelling test

1.

2.

3.

4.

5.

6.

7.

8.

Crossword - loud and soft g and c

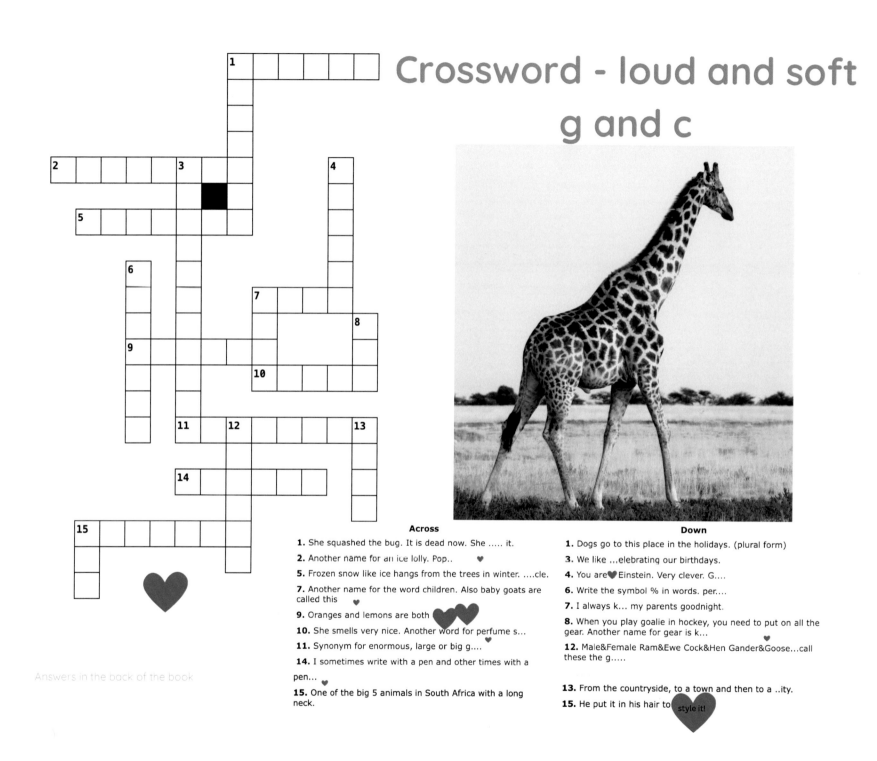

Across

1. She squashed the bug. It is dead now. She ..... it.

2. Another name for an ice lolly. Pop.. ♥

5. Frozen snow like ice hangs from the trees in winter. ....cle.

7. Another name for the word children. Also baby goats are called this ♥

9. Oranges and lemons are both ♥♥

10. She smells very nice. Another word for perfume s...

11. Synonym for enormous, large or big g.... ♥

14. I sometimes write with a pen and other times with a pen... ♥

15. One of the big 5 animals in South Africa with a long neck.

Down

1. Dogs go to this place in the holidays. (plural form)

3. We like ...elebrating our birthdays.

4. You are ♥ Einstein. Very clever. G....

6. Write the symbol % in words. per....

7. I always k... my parents goodnight.

8. When you play goalie in hockey, you need to put on all the gear. Another name for gear is k... ♥

12. Male&Female Ram&Ewe Cock&Hen Gander&Goose...call these the g.....

13. From the countryside, to a town and then to a ..ity.

15. He put it in his hair to style it!

Answers in the back of the book

F l o s s (zz) rule - revision

f l s z

If a one syllable word has only 1 vowel and ends in f, l, or s, z then you **double** the **last** letter.

moss boss sniff kiss stuff cuff bill fill chill drill glass grass cliff toss buzz fizz

This includes a two syllable word ACTING like a one syllable word.

flossing crosses kisses glasses bosses bossing grassing buzzing   *"Grassing on them to the local police."*

A few exceptions to the rule, we do learn here as they arrive early in our vocabulary list......are **gas yes this us bus plus chef**

ℓℓ

all
fall
tall
small

<u>Only one</u>

always
already
almost
although
altogether

cell

excel - to surpass others

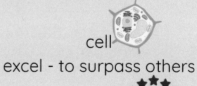

excellent

excel

excel +ing = excelling
(excelled)

The word "excel" is very unique without a double "l"

glass	hedge	stage	hatch	belch
grass	ledge	barge	match	bench
floss	wedge	large	snatch	clench
cliff	pledge	charge	scratch	drench
buff	sledge	range	patch	inch
bill	dodge	change	stitch	flinch
fill	lodge	orange	hitch	pinch
	stodge	urge	witch*	bunch
gas	budge	purge	switch	lunch
yes	fudge	surge	sketch	munch
if	nudge	binge	clutch	punch
this	smudge	cringe	crutch	much
us	grudge	plunge	twitch	stench
bus	judge	lounge		pinches
chef	fridge	twinge		
	bridge	strange	blotchy	
		merge	scratchy	
		verge		
		forge		
		gorge		
		edge		

Word bank

sink
sing
sang ←
song
singing

These words we slip in here...can be tricky for some. You can add more words like these if it is a challenging sound to spell : ding, dong, bang, ring, rang, rung, rank.
You can also make a comparison to sink sank sunk.....drink drank drunk.

Always put words in context by using it in a sentence. Refer to the same sentence every time you ask to spell the word.

Look at these words and notice the two different ways to spell the same sound. Connect to the correct picture.

tall   wall

roll   doll

toll   call

all   fall

{l}.........igh and ight

....i`ve **g**ot **h**ealthy **t**eeth

high	night	eight vs ate	lightning
hi!	knight	weight	bright**e**ning
		height	fright**e**ning
sigh	might	weigh	whit**e**ning
thigh	fright		
	fight		
write	right	mite	
right	sight	site	
	light	lite	
	bright	bite....bit	

Ask high and hi! together

The word write....refers to how little children pretend to write - write it with a "w" .....wwwww...

ate

8

I eat → I ate

- This group of words should be asked together often.
- First analyse the "ight" words together.
- Then the homophones "write" and "right".
- Next "eight" words starting with number 8 and draw the reference between weight and weigh.
- Good to bring in the word "ate" as well.
- Then follow with the "igh" sound and bring in "hi".
- Lastly the challenging words, but it is very possible to spell them correctly with stressing the "e" sound when pronouncing fright**e**ning

{l}.........igh and ight

- The boy of eight checked his weight. He weighed himself and checked his height. This highlights how the word **height belongs to the weight** family and that is why we spell it like this - even though the sound is different.

- At **night** time the **knight fights** without a **light** and no **sight** with all his **might.**

- It is important to bring in homophones once the sound is mastered. Compare mite, site and lite with might, sight and light etc. so it will be anchored in the mind. ⚓

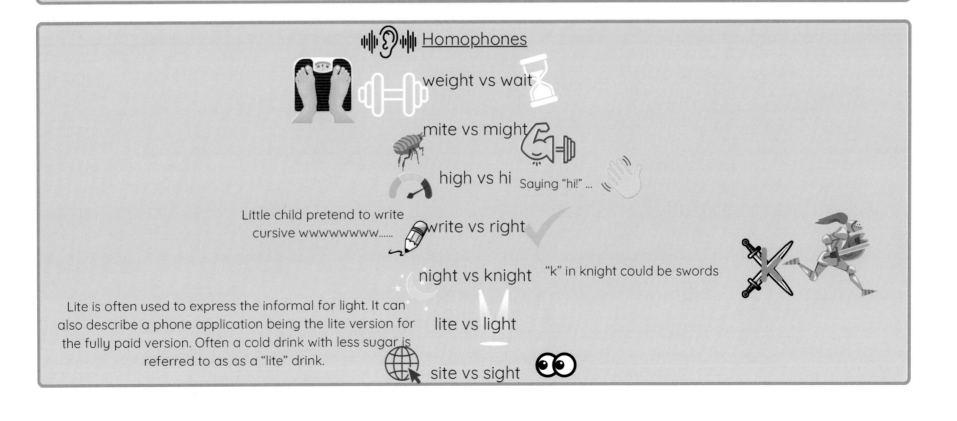

Homophones

weight vs wait

mite vs might

high vs hi Saying "hi!" ...

Little child pretend to write cursive wwwwwwww...... write vs right ✓

night vs knight "k" in knight could be swords

Lite is often used to express the informal for light. It can also describe a phone application being the lite version for the fully paid version. Often a cold drink with less sugar is referred to as as a "lite" drink. lite vs light

site vs sight

Let`s take a closer look

eight

weight

weigh

height

high

hi

Start with the word "eight" and see how it changes to "weight". "weight" and "height" do not sound the same, but are spelled the same way. They are both body measurements. "height" and "high" sound similar but are spelled differently. Then we look at the greeting "hi".

Ask to write these words together, often and for an extended period of time. Repetition is key!

{l}.........igh & ight & eight

This sentence doesn't make a lot of sense. Only for spelling purposes we want to group these words together.

The  fight in the n 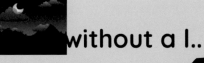 without a l.. with no s........ without fr with all m .

Write a word for each picture and check your answer below.

_____   _____

_____   _____

_____   _____

The knight fight in the night without a light with no sight without fright with all might.

A boy of 8.................
checked his ....
and after he .... himself,
he checked his ....
He can jump so .... now!

eight
weight
weighed
height
high

Word bank

*quit
*quite
*quiet

quota
quote
quilt
squash
quaint
quest
quench
quantity
squishy
squirrel
request
equips
equal
squirt
inquisitive
acquaintance
quarrel
require
queen
quay

queue

Always put words in context by putting the word in a phrasing or sentence. Use the same sentence every time you refer to that word.

Homophones

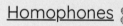

ridge
rich

- Ask ridge and rich together and talk about the meaning of these two words. If they know another language, ie french...the word in french for rich is "riche"....so no "d" sound in it. So we do something similar in English. Anchors ⚓ are so important to remind us how to spell words.

night	much	← Exceptions!!
knight	such	
might		
fright	mite	
fight	site	
right	lite	
sight	bite....bit	
light		
bright	lightning	
	brightening	
high	frightening	
hi!	whitening	
sigh	wait vs weight	
thigh	hi vs high	
	write vs right	
write	night vs knight	
right	lite vs light	
eight	ate vs eight	
weight		
height		
weigh		

To double or not to double

1 : 1 : 1 word

1 syllable

1 vowel

1 consonant

begining and end

hop

ship

add -ing -**e**d -**a**nce
-**e**st -**e**r -**a**ble
(**vowel suffix**)
<u>DOUBLE</u> the consonant of the root word!

ho**pp**ing

shi**pp**ed

add -**m**ent (-less)
(consonant suffix)
do **not** double the consonant of the root word.

shipment

---

or   a word that mimics a 1 : 1 : 1 word

When adding a **vowel suffix to a strong final syllable word** then double the consonant of the root word.

1 syllable

1 vowel

1 consonant

final syllable strong /
accent on final syllable

be<u>gin</u>	begi**nn**er
for<u>get</u>	forge**tt**ing
for<u>got</u>	forgo**tt**en
<u>gar</u>den	gardening
re<u>fer</u>	refe**rr**ing
com<u>mit</u>	commi**tt**ed
e<u>quip</u>	equi**pp**ed
pre<u>fer</u>	prefe**rr**ed

Shouting these words out loud, will give you a good indication of where the accent is.

Add consonant suffix
to a strong final syllable word
don`t double the consonant.

eg comm**it**ment

To double or not to double

1:1:1

Close up the right side and see if you can write these words without looking.

hop + ing ho**pp**ing
big + er bi**gg**er
slip + ed sli**pp**ed
bag + y ba**gg**y
(y being our cameleon - feeling like a vowel today)
fat + er fa**tt**er
compel + ed compe**ll**ed
babysit + er babysi**tt**er
control + able contro**ll**able
admit + ance admi**tt**ance

Look at the words
hoping and **hopping**
and see how they differ
in meaning -
this shows that spelling
really matters !

Let us investigate the following words...

Adding a **vowel suffix** (-ing -ish -er...) to a **silent "e"** 1:1:1 word
hope + ing ....we take away the "e" and add the suffix only

hope + **i**ng   hoping
dance + **e**r   dancer
rehearse + **a**l   rehearsal
white + **i**sh   whitish

active + **l**y   actively
The "e" stops the rootword from ending with a "illegal" letter "v"., However the suffix "ly" begins with a consonant...so we keep the "e".

What happened here?

courag**e** + ous   courag**e**ous
The "e" makes the "g" a soft sound "j". We need to keep it so it can continue to make the "g" have a soft sound.
Other examples
outrag**e**ous
advantag**e**ous
noticeable .... we keep the "e" because it has a very important job....making the "c" say "s".

To double or not to double

Explain why you double the consonant in one word and not the other word, then write the correct spelling of each word in the box.

commit   commit + ed

commit   commit + ment

hop   hop + ing

hope   hope + ing

adding -s or -es to the plural form of the word

- Most of the time we add just "s" (scoop → scoops)
- But we need a vowel in every syllable (dish → dish**e**s)

- If the word ends in a **consonant** + y, the "y" changes to an "i" and we add "es". (cher**ry** → cherr**ie**s, spy → spies)
- If the word ends in a **vowel** + y   just add an "s" (da**y** → day**s**)
- If the word ends in a **vowel** + o   add an "s" (pistachi**o** → pistahio**s**)
- If the word ends in a **consonant** + o   add an "s" **or** "es" (hero → heroes piano → pianos)
- If the word ends in f or fe   it change to v +es (wife → wives, knife → knives, loaf → loaves)
- Some words end in "f" don`t change (chef → chefs) Often the word is "borrowed" from another language).
- Irregular plurals (man → men, child → children, tooth → teeth, ice → ice, sheep → sheep, mouse → mice, foot → feet, goose → geese, people → people,   deer → deer, scissor → scissors, trousers → trousers)
- We don`t double x w y (except to change the meaning : web/Webb, mat/Matt, an/Ann, but/butt)

adding -s or -es to the plural form of the word

cars	classes	brushes	cries
frogs	kisses	eyelashes	dries
dogs	misses	splashes	flies
cats	crosses	patches	fries
birds	dishes	switches	fifties
trees	fishes	peaches	entries
ships	buses	branches	berries
animals		ostriches	bellies
buckets			babies
baskets	*Important here to refer back to the Floss Rule with exceptions!	taxes	pastries
umbrellas		boxes	sixties
roots		foxes	twenties
			hobbies
		turkeys	butterflies

* Remember the word eye with this image.

 y

e y e s

<u>Let us find the WHY</u>
Why do we write **fries** like this?
What is wrong with "fr**i**"…..ahhh!
It is "illegal" to have "i" at the end of a word unless it is borrowed from another language. "**y**" comes to the rescue! (fry)
But now we have to write the plural of fry, so we take away the "**y**" that came to the rescue, and go back to "**i**" and add "**es**"

SO COOL

Adding -s or -es to the plural form of the word

- Most of the time we add just ....   s (hats)

- If we don`t have a vowel in the syllable when we add a "s", then we add ....   es (dishes)

- If a word ends in a **consonant + y** like in cherry, then we ....   ies (cherries)

- If a word ends in a **vowel + y** like in day, then we add ....   s (days)

- If a word ends in a **vowel + o** like in pistachio, then we . add.......   s (pistachios)

- If a word ends in a **consonant + o** like in piano or hero, then we add ....   s or es (pianos or heroes)

- If a word ends in f or fe like in loaf or wife, then we ....   remove the f or fe and add ves (loaves or wives)

- What happens when we want to write the word chef in the plural form?   No change. It is a "borrowed" word. We just add s (chefs)

- What are these words called ? man ➞ men, child ➞ children, sheep ➞ sheep   Irregular plurals

Adding -s or -es to the plural form of the word

plural = more than 1 otherwise called singular

Write the plural of these words.

hero	fox	goose
echo	quiz	man
potato	horse	woman
		ice
zoo	story	person
kangaroo	fly	sheep
radio	party	foot
video	baby	tooth
bus		child
lunch	wolf	mouse
dish	leaf	deer
box	shelf	

Word ending in y + suffix »»» change "y" to "i" or not?

Word ending with a consonant

Consonant + y + ed/er/es »»»**change y to i**

cry + ed = cried
try + ed = tried
fly + es = flies
try + es = tries
carry + ed = carried

Word ending with a vowel

Vowel + y + ed/er/es »»» **keep y**

play + ed = played

The {A} sound (ay) at the end of a word: remember the reason why "y" is there. It is to rescue the "i" that cannot be at the end of a word eg. dai (day). When we add -ly, then "i" is no longer on the end of the word, so the "y" doesn`t need to help us anymore. So the "y" change back to an i. day »»» daily

lay »»» laid
say »»» said
day »»»daily

Word + y + ing »»» **keep y**

play + ing = playing
cry + ing = crying
say + ing = saying
carry + ing = carrying

Often adding the suffixes -ly and -ness we do not change the y in shyly dryly shyness dryness. However these are uncommon.

consonant tr + y + ed »»» change y to i

vowel pla + y + ed suffix »»» keep y

ing word + y + ing »»» keep y + ing

Write the plural of the word

ship	
tree	
kiss	
umbrella	
sheep	
fish	
bus	
baby	
eyelash	
fox	

Write the word with the suffix

big+er	
bag+y	
babysit +er	
commit+ment	
admit+ance	
slip+ed	
garden+ing	
forgot+en	
equip+ed	
prefer+ed	

Rewrite these sentences below with the correct spelling.

Alltogether the cheves equiped themselves with ate knifes.

They had forgoten to way the meat on the scale, allthough al of the fruit were waid.

His hight will determine how hi he can jump.

He is allways equiped for the cooking clas.

The buses weighted in the carpark for ate minutes.

Won bus had no gass.

The bus driver keeps forgeting to fil it up.

You mite find a gass station write next to the brite lite.

Word bank

peas
piece
peace
please

all
always
altogether
almost

beginner
forgetting
forgotten
gardening
referring
committed
equipped
preferred

kangaroos
potatoes
heroes
pianos
prayed
played
playing
tried
trying

where
why
what
when

tall
toll
call
doll
ball
fall

which
whitch
sandwich

wrapping
wrapped

stayed
saying
said

there
then
that

floss
buzz
cuff
ill
cell

jogging
jogged

making
made (your bed)

there
their
they`re

excel
excellent

jumping
jumped

lay an egg - laid an egg
telling a lie - past tense lied
lie down to sleep - lay down to sleep

these
those

lovelier
prettier
prettiest
loveliest

bigger
fattest

baggy

excel +ent = excellent

children (child + ren)
ostriches (o + str +i + ch + es)
(write the singular form and then add es)

lie lay laid lied
Which one is which?

Present Tense (today/now)   **Past Tense (yesterday)**

Today   Yesterday

The hens **lay** eggss   lay  laid   The hens **laid** eggs.

 **lied**

They **lie** to us. (not telling the truth)   lie   They **lied** to us.

They **lie** down to sleep.   lie  lay   They **lay** down to sleep.

Connect each word with the matching picture and to the right sentence.

The hens _ eggs

Yesterday the hens _ ten eggs.

They _ down to sleep.

Yesterday they _ down to sleep for two hours.

They never speak the truth. They often ......

Yesterday, he did not tell the truth. He ......

lie

lie

lay

laid

lied

lay

Comparative and Superlative

Discussing the spelling of the comparative and superlative form will open up an enormous bank of words.

Remember 1:1:1 rule: double the consonant if adding a vowel suffix to a 1:1:1 word.

		Comparative (er/more)	Superlative (est/most)
• One syllable	quick old	quick**er** old**er**	quick**est** old**est**
• One syllable ending in "e"	safe nice big wet	saf**er** nic**er** bigg**er** wett**er**	saf**est** nic**est** bigg**est** wettest
• Two syllables ending in "y"	heav**y** lovel**y**	heav**ier** lovel**ier**	heaviest loveliest
• **Two or more syllables**	famous	more famous	most famous
• **Irregular**	good bad	better worse	best worst

Comparative and Superlative

Write the comparative and superlative of these words.

	Comparative (er/more)	Superlative (est/most)
quick		
old		
nice		
big		
wet		
pretty		
lovely		
crunchy		
famous		
handsome		
good		
bad		
dry		
busy		
chewy		

Contractions and Apostrophe

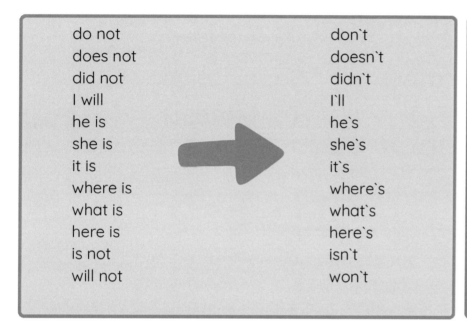

do not	don`t
does not	doesn`t
did not	didn`t
I will	I`ll
he is	he`s
she is	she`s
it is	it`s
where is	where`s
what is	what`s
here is	here`s
is not	isn`t
will not	won`t

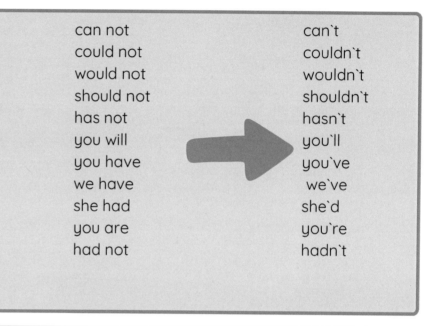

can not	can`t
could not	couldn`t
would not	wouldn`t
should not	shouldn`t
has not	hasn`t
you will	you`ll
you have	you`ve
we have	we`ve
she had	she`d
you are	you`re
had not	hadn`t

who is ➡ who`s
(different from whose)

Who is (Who`s) going to town?
Whose shoes are those?

it is ➡ it`s
(different from its)
The dog wags its tail. Its tail is long.
It`s a big dog.

This will be covered in the grammar lesson.

1 cow and his tail   the cow`s tail
2 cows and their tails   the cows` tails

BUT
Mrs Brown`s book
Mr Jones`s book

Contractions and Apostrophe

Add an apostrophe "s" or just an " ` " to the contractions below. Two of the sentences do not need correction.

1. Hes going to take his pencil to school.
2. Isnt it the cows tail that got stuck in the gate?
3. Youve brought Mr Jones book.
4. The boys shoes weren`t clean.
5. Jess cat is black.
6. The dog wags its tail.
7. Its tail is long.
8. Whos your friend?

Write the contraction.

do not	can not
does not	could not
did not	would not
I will	should not
he is	has not
she is	you will
it is	you have
where is	who is
what is	we have
here is	
is not	

A few more sounds to look at

"ice" making the sound {ll}s
What makes the "c" sound soft like a "s"?
The "e" (or "i" or "y") that follows the "c".

<u>Remember</u> "c" and "g" followed by i e   y   gives us a **soft** sound!

ize

capsize

maize

prize

seize

size

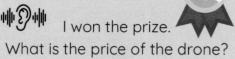
I won the prize.
What is the price of the drone?

ice

ice

rice

lice

mice

nice

dice

dice is the plural form of 1 die

ace

ace

face 😊

place

grace

aze

maze

blaze

froze

graze
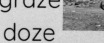

doze

Connect the each word with the matching picture and sentence

The cows gr.... in the green fields.

grace

She did not deal with him harshly. She was very kind and was showing him a lot of gr....

graze

The doctor prescribed the right do..... of medicine for your age.

dose

My grandmother and grandfather do.... off in the afternoons.

doze

Every morning they ri..... early for breakfast.

rise

I eat a lot of ri.... when I am in Thailand.

rice

price   prize   surprise

Look at these words carefully.

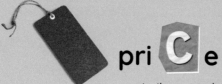

pri C e

What is the price of that dress? **c**ost - price tag

pri Z e

He won a prize for being so good at spelling!

surpri S e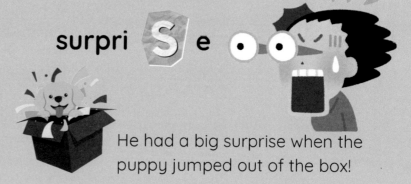

He had a big surprise when the
puppy jumped out of the box!

Connect each word to the right picture

price   prize   surprise

 whiskers

wh

 whole

 wheel

 whine

 whisper

 whales

 wheat

 whisk

 whistle

white

whether
weather

Weather is written with an "e" and "a" - we get sun and rain - it changes.

wh w or wr

wreck

wrong

wrap

wrapping

unwrapped

wriggle

wren

whiskers

wheel

whisper

whisk

white

world

watch

wasp

wallet

wish

There is a mole in the hole, but that is a **whole** different story.

Do not **whine** about the **wine**.

Are there **whales** in **Wales**?

Add c or z or s   Add w or wh or wr

gra_e	i_e	_eck	_iggle
gra_e	li_e	_asp	_en
a_e	capsi_e	_ine	_allet
fro_e	ni_e	_ine	-ong
fa_e	mai_e	_iskers	-eel
pla_e	ri_e	_ales	-apping
no_e	ri_e	_ales	-isper
do_e	pri_e	-orld	-ite
do_e	pri_e	-isk	-atch
ro_e	surpri_e	_ap	un_apped
bla_e	si_e		
di_e	mi_e		
	sei_e		

Mark right or wrong for each sentence. Circle the wrong words.

✔   ✗

Whales expel air from their blowholes.
Wales expel air from their blowwhols.

He whines often about not having enough red wine in his glass.
He wines often about not having enough red whine in his glass.

The cat`s wite wiskers riggles when I wisper in it`s ear.
The cat`s white whiskers wriggle when I whisper in its ear.

His face froze when he got stuck in the maze with mice running around his feet.
His fase frose when he got stuck in the mase with mise running around his feet.

Spelling test

1. _____

2. _____

3. _____

4. _____

5. _____

6. _____

7. _____

8. _____

....and there was silence!

Some words have silent letters that we do not pronounce.

silent b

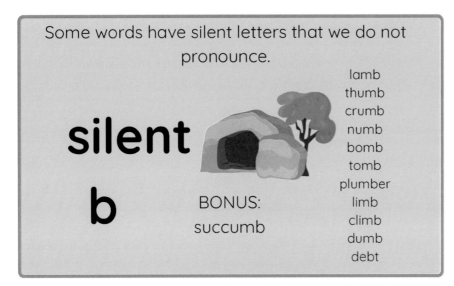

lamb
thumb
crumb
numb
bomb
tomb
plumber
limb
climb
dumb
debt

BONUS:
succumb

silent k g t

often
knot
knock
know
knee
knife
knight
knuckle

gnash
gnaw
gnome
sign
resign
design

Often the sound "f" is written with a "ph". These words have a different origin. They do indeed have a story of how they came into existence in the English language.

ph

photo
photograph
graph
elephant
telephone
physical
alphabet

phrase
apostrophe
triumph
orphan
nephew
phlegm
hyphen

emphasis
geography
paragraph
pharmacy
sphere
phobia

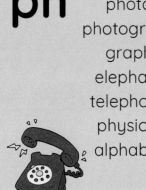

sc
you only hear "s"

homophones
scent and sent and cent
seen and scene

scenic
scenario
scenery
fascinate

scene
science
scissors
muscle
ascend
descend
transcend
disciple
discipline
obscene
adolescent
fluorescent

....and there was silence!

silent

b

lamb
thumb
crumb
numb
bomb
tomb

plumber
limb
climb
dumb
debt

BONUS:
succumb

Write the words of the following pictures on the next page and check if you have written them correctly.

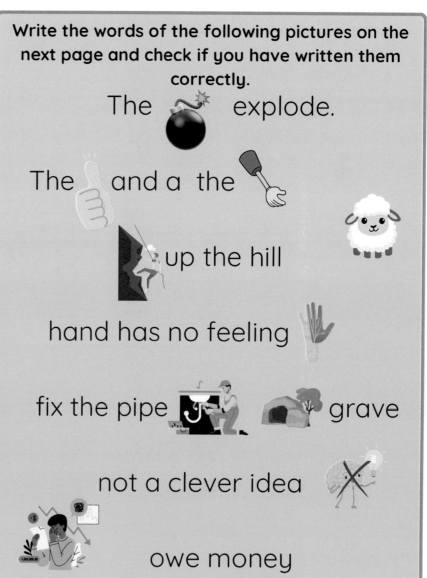

The 🧨 explode.

The 👍 and a the 🔨

🧗 up the hill 🐑

hand has no feeling 🖐

fix the pipe 🚰 🪦 grave

not a clever idea 🧠

owe money 💸

Finish writing these words

bo

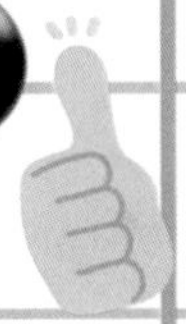

th

li

la

cl

nu

plu

to

du

de

....and there was silence!

silent	silly phrases / rewrite them
k g t	gnashing gnome gnaw (nibble) the straw
	_____
	sign your design
	_____
	often knock with your knuckle not your knee
	_____
	a knight knows how to undo a knot with a knife
	_____

....and there was silence!

ph

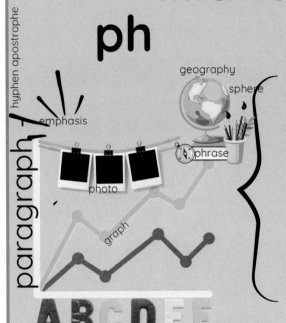

hyphen apostrophe

paragraph

emphasis

photo

graph

alphabet

ABCDEF

geography

sphere

phrase

{
photo
photograph
telephone
graph
phrase
apostrophe
hyphen
alphabet
paragraph
emphasis
geography
sphere
}
**Writing
Drawing
Communicating**

Sometimes words with the sound "f"in them, are written with a "ph". These words often are of greek origin. They do indeed have a story of how they came into existence in the English language.

{
orphan
nephew
elephant
}
The word nephew is derived from the French word neveu which is derived from the Latin nepos Same with nece - niece.

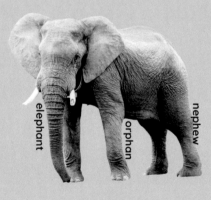

elephant

orphan

nephew

phlegm

physical

phobia
(irrational or uncontrollable fear)

philosophical

pharmacy

triumph

{
phlegm
physical
pharmacy
phobia
triumph
philosophical
}
Wellbeing

I went to the pharmacy because I had physical phlegm.
You have to be philosophical about your phobias, if you want to triumph.

....and there was silence!

sc
you only hear "s"

The "sc" spelling comes from the Latin spelling via the French language.
There is nothing complicated about English spelling. It is just that some words have a different origin than others.

scent
ascend
descend
transcend
(surpass - transcend all understanding)

Fill in the words

4. ....

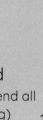 

1. ....

3. ....

2. ....

1. ascend
2. transcend
3. descend
4. scent

scene
scenic
scenario
scenery

scenic scene scenery scenario

disciple **dis + ci+ ple**
discipline **dis + ci+ pline**

discipline yourself to add an "e" to the end of discipline

science
scientist
scissors
muscle
obscene
(a lot)

obscene amount of muscle

science scientist scissors

<u>Homophones</u>
scent and sent and cent
seen and scene

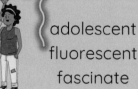

adolescent
fluorescent
fascinate

a + do + le + scent
fluo + re + scent

Adolescents are fascinated by fluorescent lights.

Write the letters

b	b	k	sc
thum _	lam _	_ nock	__ ent
bom _	crum _	_ not	__ ene
clim _	plum _ er	_ now	__ ience
de _ t	lim _	_ new	__ issors
num _	succum _	_ nowledge	mu __ le
g	g	_ nee	a __ end
_ nome	resi _ n	_ nife	de __ end
si _n	_ nash	_ night	dis _ ipline
si _nature	_ naw	_ nuckle	__ enery

Word search

```
s i g h t t b t x s t p m i e
c g t t h b m h r h w e i g h
b v n g y e o g g u n x n r e
s r i a n d b i t a m c g a l
b e i e s g f r h j k n i p k
h m t g s h i f g k o f s h c
p f u i h t f s i m n d e i u
o k g d c t h j e t b o d g n
o h k n o t r g w r h m c h k
t h u m b t h g i u i g u k n
l i m b h g i h t n i n i n o
n g i s a r b b k h k a a n w
e f i n k m m n m d g w o j k
t x t y a o e t b b m i l c i
n j s l t e b m u r c x e l k
```

climb	bright	bomb
design	debt	crumb
fight	eight	dumb
gnaw	gnash	fright
height	graph	gnome
knife	knee	high
knock	knight	knight
knuckle	know	knot
numb	limb	lamb
sigh	resign	often
thigh	sign	sight
weigh	tomb	thumb
		weight

capsize	ice	ace	maze	lamb	photo	scenic
maize	rice	face	blaze	thumb	photograph	scenario
prize	lice	place	froze	crumb	graph	scenery
seize	mice	grace	graze	numb	elephant	fascinate
size	nice		doze	bomb	telephone	
	dice			tomb	physical	
price				plumber	alphabet	scent
prize				limb		scene
surprise				climb		science
				dumb		scissors
				debt		muscle
				BONUS:	phrase	ascend
wreck	whiskers	gnash		succumb	apostrophe	descend
wrong	wheel	gnaw		(overcome)	triumph	transcend
wrap	whisper	gnome		(fail to resist	orphan	disciple
wrapping	whisk	sign		pressure)	nephew	discipline
unwrapped	white	resign			phlegm	obscene
wriggle		design			hyphen	adolescent
wren						fluorescent
	wine					
	whine	often				scent
	hole	knot			emphasis	sent
	whole	knock			geography	cent
	whales	know			paragraph	
	Wales	knee			pharmacy	
world		knife			sphere phobia	
watch		knight				
wasp		knuckle				
wallet						

Word bank

Mark the mistakes and rewrite the correct spelling of the words afterwards

I had a telefone call from an adolesent in the ciense department explaining where the plummer found the bom.

The broken nome in the garden was a sine that the hooligans climed over the fence.

The sinetist used a nife and sissors to cut out a sfere for the giogrefy lesson.

The man asended up the mountain. The senery was beautiful and transended his expectations. He decended down the mountain with an elefant that had an injured lim.

He wrote a paragraf without using apostrofis and hifins.

You need to go to the farmacy and ask them to look at your thum injury.

There was nawing and nashiing of teeth when my nefew took on the lion.

We need to now how ofen the boy broke his nuckles and nees.

Can you scend the sent so I can smell it and send you money in the form of sents?

Please take some fotografs of your senic trip.

Rewrite the correct spelling of the words below

Answers
dge ge tch or ch

surge	binge	urge
lounge	range	catch
nudge	twitch	stage
orange	which	fridge
sledge	witch	bridge
crutch	cringe	edge
grudge	twinge	punch
judge	wedge	pinch
bench	lunge	dodge
latch	rich	snatch
stitch	ridge	fudge
drench	large	sledge
plunge	such	much

Answers -ge/dge & ch/tch

The witch with her huge crooked nose was sitting in her lounge. The only way to escape was over a bridge and over the hedge.

Not far from there, lived a knight who could fight in the night with all his might. Even in the bright light he could punch and scratch. The witch was no match for him.

I think it was her height and her weight that was the biggest problem. The knight was only eight years old. He was much younger than the strange old lady.

Answers -where why what they their there

Where are you going on holiday?

Why would you not take your teddy with you?

When will you be back?

They`re coming with us to the beach.

Will you be going to their party?

There are so many sports we can play on the beach.

Which of those two friends do you play ball with?

The witch is eating her sandwich.

That is an interesting question to ask.

Their school is near the city.

There is a big house near the school.

Answers

loud g or c	soft g (j) or c ("s")
goat	gel
guess	giant
cat	cycle
cot	gym
game	fence
	large
	rescue

1 killed

2 popsicle

3 celebration

4 genius

5 icicles

6 percent

7 kids

8 kit

9 citrus

10 scent

11 gigantic

12 gender

13 city

14 pencil

15 giraffe

16 gel

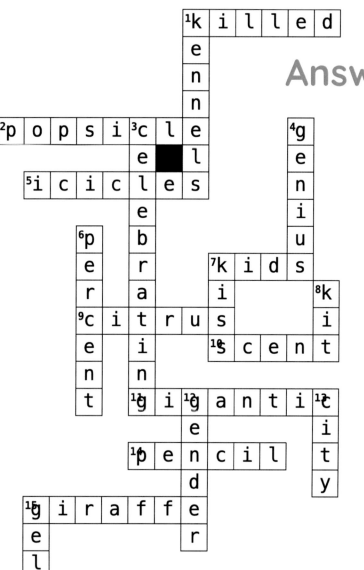

Adding -s or -es to the plural form of the word

Answers

hero	heroes	fox	foxes	goose	geese
echo	echoes	quiz	quizzes	man	men
potato	potatoes	horse	horses	woman	women
				ice	ice
zoo	zoos	story	stories	person	people
kangaroo	kangaroos	fly	flies	sheep	sheep
radio	radios	party	parties	foot	feet
video	videos	baby	babies	tooth	teeth
bus	buses			child	children
lunch	lunches	wolf	wolves	mouse	mice
dish	dishes	leaf	leaves	deer	deer
box	boxes	shelf	shelves		

Answers - plural of the word

Answers - the word with the suffix

ship	ships
tree	trees
kiss	kisses
umbrella	umbrellas
wife	wives
fish	fishes
bus	buses
baby	babies
eyelash	eyelashes
fox	foxes

big+er	bigger
bag+y	baggy
babysit +er	babysitter
commit+ment	commitment
admit+ance	admittance
slip+ed	slipped
garden+ing	gardening
forgot+en	forgotten
equip+ed	equipped
prefer+ed	preferred

Answers - Chefs with knives

Altogether the chefs equipped themselves with eight knives.

They had forgotten to weigh the meat on the scale, although all of the fruit were weighed.

His height will determine how high he can jump.

He is always equipped for the cooking class.

The buses waited in the carpark for eight minutes.

One bus had no gas.

The bus driver keeps forgetting to fill it up.

You might find a gas station right next to the bright light.

Comparative and Superlative

Answers

	Comparative (er/more)	Superlative (est/most)
quick	quicker	quickest
old	older	oldest
nice	nicer	nicest
big	bigger	biggest
wet	wetter	wettest
pretty	prettier	prettiest
lovely	lovelier	loveliest
crunchy	crunchier	crunchiest
famous	more famous	most famous
handsome	more handsome	most handsome
good	better	best
bad	worse	worst
dry	drier	driest
busy	busier	busiest
chewy	chewier	chewiest

Answers

1. He`s going to take his pencil to school.
2. Isn`t it the cow`s tail that got stuck in the gate?
3. You`ve brought Mr Jones`s book.
4. The boy`s shoes wasn`t clean.
5. Jess`s cat is black.
6. The dog wags its tail.
7. Its tail is long.
8. Who`s your friend?

don`t	can`t
doesn`t	couldn`t
didn`t	wouldn`t
I`ll	shouldn`t
he`s	hasn`t
she`s	you`ll
it`s	you`ve
where`s	who`s
what`s	we`ve
here`s	
isn`t	

Answers

c or z or s

grace	ice
graze	lice
ace	capsize
froze	nice
face	maize
place	rice
nose	rise
dose	price
doze	prize
rose	surprise
blaze	size
dice	mice
	seize

w or wh or wr

wreck	wriggle
wasp	wren
wine	wallet
whine	wrong
whiskers	wheel
whales	wrapping
Wales	whisper
world	white
whisk	watch
wrap	unwrapped

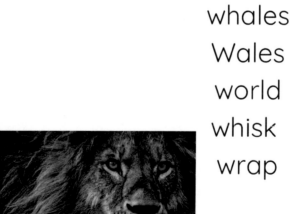

Answer - silent letters we do not hear

I had a telephone call from an adolescent in the science department explaining where the plumber found the bomb.

The broken gnome in the garden was a sign that the hooligans had climbed over the fence.

The scientist used a knife and scissors to cut out a sphere for the geography lesson.

The man ascended up the mountain. The scenery was beautiful and transcended his expectations. He decended down the mountain with an elephant that had an injured limb.

He wrote a paragraph without using apostrophes and hyphens.

You need to go to the pharmacy and ask them to look at your thumb injury..

There was gnawing and gnashing of teeth when my nephew took on the lion.

We need to know how often the boy broke his knuckles and knees.

Can you send the scent so I can smell it and send you money in the form of cents?

Please take some photographs of your scenic trip.

A Logical Approach to Spelling

You can contact us by email
info@logicalapproachtolearning.com
2024 Jurina Dean
You can follow us on Instagram logicalapproachtospelling

Milton Keynes UK
Ingram Content Group UK Ltd.
UKRC031101021124
450368UK00001B/2